YOUR KNOWLEDGE HAS VALUE

- We will publish your bachelor's and master's thesis, essays and papers

- Your own eBook and book - sold worldwide in all relevant shops

- Earn money with each sale

Upload your text at www.GRIN.com and publish for free

Mark Schauer

The ethics of starvation

GRIN Verlag

Bibliografische Information der Deutschen Nationalbibliothek:

Die Deutsche Bibliothek verzeichnet diese Publikation in der Deutschen National-
bibliografie; detaillierte bibliografische Daten sind im Internet über http://dnb.d-
nb.de/ abrufbar.

Imprint:

Copyright © 2009 GRIN Verlag GmbH
Druck und Bindung: Books on Demand GmbH, Norderstedt Germany
ISBN: 978-3-656-46812-7

GRIN - Your knowledge has value

Der GRIN Verlag publiziert seit 1998 wissenschaftliche Arbeiten von Studenten, Hochschullehrern und anderen Akademikern als eBook und gedrucktes Buch. Die Verlagswebsite www.grin.com ist die ideale Plattform zur Veröffentlichung von Hausarbeiten, Abschlussarbeiten, wissenschaftlichen Aufsätzen, Dissertationen und Fachbüchern.

Visit us on the internet:

http://www.grin.com/

http://www.facebook.com/grincom

http://www.twitter.com/grin_com

Mark Schauer

Spring 2009

The study of ethics deals with the largest questions of the human condition. The most important of these are those that concern the most basic requirement of existence: enough nourishment and nutrition to sustain life. Though food insecurity exists in the United States, more individuals in this country suffer the ill effects of too much food consumption than starve. This is usually not the case in the developing countries of the Third World, nor in undeveloped countries with little or no chance of ever obtaining a standard of living remotely comparable to that of the industrialized nations. LaFollette asks, "Are we obligated to do more than not harm foreigners?" (LaFollette 611)[1] And, for that matter, are we obligated to help the people of nations in which doing so would have no political benefits for our nation? Finally, is standing by and allowing a famine to claim millions of lives as ethically reprehensible as actively causing the same number of deaths?

Since Joseph Stalin demonstrated the effectiveness of eliminating undesirable peoples through famines, most of the world has come to accept that passively allowing others to die by starvation is an unethical and immoral act. You are more likely to find an elected official endorsing the use of nuclear weapons than suggesting that their nation's enemies be deliberately starved. Anti-hunger campaigns are among the world's most well-known charities. The Universal Declaration of Human Rights holds that access to food is a basic and unalienable human right, and no serious public figure of any political persuasion in the western world would openly express anything but sympathy for those who lack sufficient food. Yet, according to Pogge, 790 million of the world's people suffer this unenviable condition, and a third of human deaths are poverty-related. (LaFollette 633) Pogge suggests that this is systemic, caused by the economic order imposed by strong nations, who "distribute the planet's abundant wealth amongst themselves" and "in collaboration with the

---

[1] Some would say that the Judeo-Christian tradition suggests we are under no such obligation. The Old Testament is replete with instances of double standards for foreigners and those of your own nation. God commanded the Israelites not to kill (or murder) on Mt. Sinai, but later told them to invade Canaan and kill as many Canaanites as possible. Jesus' complimentary comments about Samaritans notwithstanding, aggression was usually projected outward onto those who were different.

1

ruling elites of the poor countries coercively exclude the poor from a proportional resource share." (LaFollette 637) This is self-evident to anyone with a rudimentary knowledge of the major events of world history and average reasoning skills. Yet even a sensitive western liberal like Pogge declines to call for radical alterations in this state of affairs— instead, his "moderate proposal" suggests a modest tax on resource consumption that would annually raise less than the defense budget of the United States. (LaFollette 638-39) This money would be equivalent to $250 a year for everyone below the international poverty line, a dollar figure he asserts would be a miraculous windfall to the poorest of the poor. (LaFollette 639)

An opposing view is expressed by John Arthur, who holds that the current capitalist system is the only vehicle by which an end to starvation and poverty can be delivered, and that a suggestion like Pogge's violates the 'just desert' aspect any good moral code should have. (LaFollette 630) Redistributing money to the poor (even, evidently, a very modest amount) constitutes a disincentive toward working as hard as you possibly can, which would result in a lower standard of living for everyone. It also, in his view, provides a rationalization for theft from wealthy people or institutions, and such disrespect for property rights is also a disincentive toward work and responsibility. (LaFollette 630) Early in his piece, Arthur illustrates his 'just desert' philosophy with the example of Nazi war criminals who deserved punishment. These individuals were punished—many of the worst were executed. Yet they were not starved. And using such an illustration in a piece putatively concerned with famine relief is the brittlest of straw men.

Peter Singer's passionate and impressively reasoned analysis of the famine in East Bengal in the early 1970s is an outstanding platform from which to address the moral duties associated with preventing world hunger. He goes to the heart of the system when he decries the relief effort being described as charity, for when, "giving money is regarded as an act of charity, it is not thought that there is anything wrong with not giving. The charitable man may be praised, but the man who is not charitable is not condemned." (LaFollette 616) He blasts those who conspicuously consume in the face of massive starvation, buttresses his plea with searing quotes from Thomas

Aquinas and the *Decretum Gratiani*, and reasserts that famine is an extreme crisis that should be treated as such.

Key to all of this, though, is the natural world that surrounds us. Rolston observes that "humans now control 40 percent of the planet's land based primary net productivity" and that 35 percent of the Earth's land has now become degraded." (LaFollette 653) Though delivering the world's poorest citizens from starvation is an attainable goal, producing enough food to provide a standard of living comparable to the West's is not. Rolston also observes that efforts to preserve the world's most fragile ecosystems are doomed when the people in them are living in extreme poverty, and that the false hope of selling a poor nation's natural resources to the industrialized world will only bring sufficient prosperity to stave off starvation until the mineral wealth has been depleted. (LaFollette 652) Rolston believes the argument over whether or not we have an obligation to feed the poor will be moot if overpopulation burdens humanity beyond its ability to feed itself. Granted, this fear is not new. Humanity has endured through many famines, and revolutionary advances in agricultural practices and the development of hybrid crops in the 20th century paid handsome dividends to a hungry world— albeit in the form of aid packages from the west that often came with strings that benefited the wealthy attached. But yet, the world has not seen an uninterrupted advancement in technological progress, of which food is the building block— the "Dark Age" enveloped Europe when the advanced plant genetics and animal husbandry techniques of the Western Roman Empire were lost along with its collapse in the 5th century AD. The Romans, it should be added, were not particularly concerned with feeding non-Romans in foreign lands, and were brought down by peoples who were their technological inferiors.

Works Cited

LaFollette, Hugh, ed. Ethics in Practice. Malden, Massachusetts: Blackwell, 2007. 3rd ed.